SkillAbilities
FOR YOUTH MINISTRY

Youth in Charge

How To Develop Youth Leadership

by Jeff Huber and Tami Bradshaw

ABINGDON PRESS
Nashville, Tennessee

About the Writers
Jeff Huber is minister to youth and their families at Calvary United Methodist Church and Tami Bradshaw serves as youth director and coordinator of special ministries at East United Methodist Church in Colorado Springs, Colorado. Jeff and Tami have been married five years and enjoy seeing movies, hanging out with their cat Smoky Jo, and going for long walks in the mountains with their dog Ginger.

Acknowledgments
The youth and adults of Calvary and East United Methodist Churches, Colorado
  Springs, Colorado
Youth workers in the Rocky Mountain Conference of The United Methodist Church
To Crys for your faith and trust in us!

SKILLABILITIES FOR YOUTH WORKERS
Youth in Charge:
How to Develop Youth Leadership
Volume 2

SKILLABILITIES FOR YOUTH WORKERS, Volume 2
(ISBN 0-687-06200-4) An official resource for The United Methodist Church prepared by The General Board of Discipleship through Teaching and Study Resources and published by Abingdon Press, The United Methodist Publishing House, 201 Eighth Avenue South, P.O. Box 801, Nashville, TN 37202-0801. Copyright © 1997 Abingdon Press. All rights reserved. Printed in the United States of America.

To order copies of this publication, call 800-672-1789 from 7:00–6:30 (Central Time) Monday–Friday and 9–5:00 Saturday. Telecommunication Device for the Deaf/Telex Telephone: 800-227-4091. Automated order system is available after office hours.

For permission to reproduce any material in this publication, call 615-749-6421 or write to Permissions Office, 201 Eighth Avenue South, P.O. Box 801, Nashville, TN 37202-0801.

EDITORIAL AND DESIGN TEAM
Editor: Crystal A. Zinkiewicz
Production Editor: Susan Simmons
Design Manager: Phillip D. Francis
Designer: Diana Maio & Brooks Harper
Cover Design: Diana Maio
  & Phillip D. Francis

ADMINISTRATIVE TEAM
Publisher: Neil M. Alexander
Vice President: Harriett Jane Olson
**Executive Editor, Teaching and Study
  Resources:** Duane A. Ewers
Editor of Youth Resources:
  M. Steven Games

CONTENTS

page

BEFORE YOU PROCEED, READ . . .   4
What you need to know before you go on.

WHY DO THIS?   5
How do your youth, adults, and church benefit?

WHAT'S THE WORD?   10
Bible passages about the gift of leadership.

WHAT'S THE CURRENT STATUS?   12
What is your church's "youth pulse"?

LET'S DO IT!   15
13 ways to get youth and adults excited about youth being in leadership.

LET'S PLAN IT!   25
Specific strategies for planning with youth.

LET'S LEAD IT!   38
7 important traits of leadership.

LET'S KEEP IT GOING!   42
12 hints to keep your ministry youth-led and youth-planned.

TROUBLESHOOTING   50
11 common problems and prescriptions to cure them.

MINI-WORKSHOP FOR LEADERS   58
Leadership training for youth and adults.

THE BIG PICTURE   71
How does this SkillAbility fit in? What's next? Who's there to help?

BEFORE YOU PROCEED, READ...

Our assumptions:

Churches come in all different shapes and sizes. There is no one solution, program, or structure that will work for every church in developing youth leadership or planning with youth.

Youth ministry is more than a series of programs or an annex of the local congregation—it is an integral part of the body of Christ.

Our hope:

That you will find something here from our experiences that you can use effectively for your particular ministry with youth.

WHY DO THIS?

The Goal:

To develop a comprehensive ministry with youth that enables all persons in the church to recognize and use the **unique leadership gifts** young people bring to the present and future body of Christ.

BENEFITS TO YOUTH

Youth Need Assets

Search Institute has discovered and defined **40 key assets** that make a difference in the quality of a young person's life now and later. Some that relate to youth being in leadership are:

HIGH EXPECTATIONS   **Asset #16**
Adults press young persons to achieve.

PLANNING AND DECISION-MAKING   **Asset #32**
Youth have skills to plan ahead and make choices.

SENSE OF PURPOSE   **Asset #39**
Youth sense "my life has a purpose."

POSITIVE VIEW OF PERSONAL FUTURE   **Asset #40**
Youth are optimistic about their personal future.

OFFERING

Youth realize that what they have to give is a ministry.

OWNERSHIP

It's their ministry, so they're more likely to be invested in it and to show up for youth functions!

OPPORTUNITY

Planning and carrying out ministries and other functions help youth learn and develop leadership skills.

BENEFITS TO ADULTS

Adults don't have
to do all the work!

Youth are more likely
to **discipline
themselves**
if it's their ministry.

BENEFITS TO THE CHURCH

Persons begin to take seriously the Christian understanding that all are baptized into ministry and have an important role in the church.

If young people get a chance to lead now, they are more likely to continue to be in leadership roles as they become adults.

Youth can **energize a congregation** through their enthusiasm and creativity!

So be forewarned!

WHAT'S THE WORD ?

---

3 biblical images touch on the importance of youth being in leadership in the church—

1 Corinthians 12:4–11
Many Gifts/One Spirit

Paul reminds us that all persons have a gift to share, no matter their age or size. Whatever your gift, as part of the body of Christ, God calls you to use it to build up the children of God and change the world. Whether your gift is caring for others, or leading a meeting, or putting together a calendar, you are a vital part of your youth ministry.

Matthew 25:14–30
The Parable of the Talents

Recognize that all churches, no matter their style or size, are given talents. Some churches have one talent; some others, five. In other words some churches have lots of resources; some have few. Jesus' point is that no matter how many talents a church may have it must use them and not "bury them in the ground." If we begin to view our youth as talents in our church, we can no longer bury or ignore them but instead can invest in them, using what we have to serve God.

1 Samuel 3:1–10
God Calls Young Samuel

This story of Samuel vividly depicts God choosing a young person to be in leadership. Notice too in this story that Samuel is unsure he is really being called by God. It is only when his mentor, Eli, encourages him that Samuel can recognize God's voice and know that God is calling out to him to share his gifts, use his talents, and lead God's people.

Where are youth already in leadership in your congregation?

How many times a year do youth serve as:

Liturgists _____

Ushers _____

Greeters _____

Music leaders or soloists _____

Preachers _____

Sunday school or
vacation Bible school teachers
or assistants _____

Helpers for special
church programs _____

What committees do youth serve on?

Trustees or building _____

Staff parish or personnel _____

Finance or treasury _____

Education or Sunday school _____

Missions or outreach _____

Evangelism or visitation _____

Other _____

What other ministries, such as mission trips, are youth involved in?

How well are youth naturally integrated into the leadership of your youth ministry?

Do you have a more formal structure, such as a Youth Council or Youth Leadership Team that gives youth opportunities for planning and leading? (A formal structure is not a requirement.)

Youth may already be leading. How often are they recognized and affirmed for their leadership?

Do youth have opportunities to genuinely lead, or are they just filling positions with no real chance to do anything?

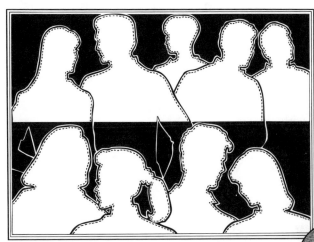

What's the Current Status?

Is your current youth ministry led by all adults? all youth? a combination of both?

Do you truly trust youth to lead?

Do you trust youth enough to let them fail and learn from their mistakes? Or do you "rescue" youth without taking time to allow them to learn and grow?

Do adult voices drown out those of the youth?

Which adults in your church will work with youth to make sure their voice is heard?

What specific strategies does your church have for offering leadership training and development for adults and for youth?

LET'S DO IT!

13 Ways to Get Youth and Adults Excited About Youth Being in Leadership

1 Get Youth Up Front in Worship

Work with your pastor to to do this. You can suggest that the youth act out a Bible story or do a skit that helps emphasize your pastor's sermon for the day. You also can help get youth signed up to be ushers, greeters, and liturgists in your church's worship experiences.

2 Create a Theme

Get potential youth and adult leaders to work together to develop a theme for the year, such as:

- GRACE—Growing Relationships After Christ's Example
- Come to the EDGE—Every Day God is Exciting
- CLIFF—Community Living In Faith and Friendship
- Or use a song or Bible passage as a theme. Just make it short and to the point—no more than seven words.

BRAINSTORM to develop a theme. Divide into smaller groups if needed. The only rule is that the theme must somehow describe what you want your youth ministry to be. Give your youth and adults something to be excited about!

HAVE AN ART CONTEST to create a logo for the theme. Put the logo on T-shirts, use it on letterhead, or paint it on the wall in your youth room! Give the winner a free T-shirt adorned with the new logo!

3 Set Goals for the Year

Work with the youth leaders to give the group something to rally around. Then make sure everyone knows about the goal. Some examples are

- **Have 5 new youth come to youth group each month.**
- **Take 20 youth on a summer mission trip.**
- **Raise $100 for a local charity.**
- **Have youth lead worship 4 Sundays a year.**

When setting goals, remember to make them

MEASURABLE
SPECIFIC
ATTAINABLE
EXCITING!!

At the end of the year, celebrate the goals you've reached and recommit or rework the ones you did not reach.

4 Look for Models

Go visit (road trip) a youth group that has youth in
leadership so your youth and adults can see youth
leading in action. Once they see it they will be motivated to
figure out how they can be in leadership in their church.

5 Seek Out Training

Take several potential youth leaders to a leadership training
event for youth.

6 Invite a Guest Trainer

Have a church member who specializes in leadership
training in the corporate world speak or lead youth group
some night. Be sure your guest also talks about how faith
is important in his or her work.

7 Apply for the Team

Have youth and adults apply to be a part of your leadership team. This process makes it a privilege to be in leadership.

SAMPLE
Youth Leadership Position Application

All persons in the Youth MALT (Ministry Area Leadership Team) are role models for the rest of the group. They are expected to act responsibly and with maturity at all youth events. It is also expected that youth who hold positions in the Youth MALT will remain active in the youth group throughout the school year and make every attempt to be present at all Youth MALT meetings.

The following positions will be chosen for the Youth MALT. Please number your choices 1 through 3, with 1 being your most preferred position.

____ Co-Coordinators (4): 2 each from Jr. High and Sr. High
____ Treasurer (1): from Sr. High
____ Fundraising Coordinators (2): 1 each from Sr. High and Jr. High
____ Newsletter Editors (3): 2 from Sr. High and 1 from Jr. High
____ At-Large Representatives—No limit

Persons interested in the positions shall apply using this form and shall be chosen by a nominating committee comprised of the pastor, one youth each from Junior High and Senior High, one sponsor, and one parent.

This nominating committee will be persons from the current Youth MALT. The entire slate of persons nominated for titled positions in the Youth MALT will be recognized on Youth Sunday at worship.

Applications for this term are due _____
Term of office is from June 1 to May 31.

Please answer the questions on the reverse side of this application to the best of your ability and return to _____ by the date listed above. You may use another sheet if necessary.

NAME:_____
GRADE:_____

ADDRESS:_____
PHONE:_____
SCHOOL:_____

Why do you desire this position?

What is most important to you about being a Christian?

What qualities and/or experiences have you had that will help you in this position?

If you've been on the MALT in the past, what suggestions would you make for improvement?

What other activities are you involved in, either at school, work, or other? Will these allow you the time you need for this position?

I,_____, recognize the importance and responsibility of being a member of the Youth MALT and promise to uphold my commitment throughout the term to the best of my ability. If I find at any point in the year that I will be unable to continue as part of the Youth MALT, I will notify the youth group either in written or verbal form. I understand that other members of the Youth MALT will hold me accountable to this promise.

Signed:_____ Date:_____

Parent's signature noting your commitment:

Signed:_____
Date:_____

8 Recognize the Team

Honor your youth leadership team at least once a year in worship, using a litany such as this.

Youth Leaders: Gracious God, as leaders we have come to this place and time, knowing you have called us by name. But there are times when we will not be sure . . .

Congregation: Give assurance to these leaders, the ones you have chosen.

Youth Leaders: As we begin this journey to lead your people, there will be many distractions and it will be hard to hear your voice . . .

Congregation: Give focus and patience to these leaders, the ones you have chosen.

Youth Leaders: When we make decisions, we may be unsure that we are doing the right thing . . .

Congregation: Give conviction and courage to these leaders, the ones you have chosen.

Youth Leaders: Sometimes leading is hard, and we will get tired and weary . . .

Congregation: Give strength and endurance to these leaders, the ones you have chosen.

Youth Leaders: Mostly, God, we want people to see in our actions that we are leaders with faith . . .

Congregation: Give hope and love to these leaders, the ones you have chosen.

All: In all that we say and do, whether we are leading or following, help us to remember that you walk beside us, dear God, and you call us each to seek justice, love, and kindness and to walk humbly with you. Amen.

9 Find Leadership Mentors

Intentionally build relationships between adults who are leaders in the church and youth who need mentors. One way to do this is to assign interested youth to work with the chair or head of different committees so they can learn about that area of the church. The adults might even let the youth lead a meeting so they can get a feel for it!

10 Celebrate Successes!

When youth plan an event that works, celebrate it. Take that opportunity to also point out ways youth are already in leadership. Advertise the information from the survey in the previous chapter in your church newsletter or worship bulletin or post it on a bulletin board. Add pictures of youth leading their ministry.

11 Spread the Word

Have several youth develop a newsletter just for youth, with articles by youth about youth leading their ministry.

12 See and Do BIG Time

Take several youth to your church's denominational governing event. Not only can they observe, but they may also find ways to participate.

13 Recognize Spiritual Gifts

Give your youth and adults the Spiritual Gifts Test (page 63) to help determine what gifts they possess. Talk with everyone about how they might use their gifts in ministry. Celebrate those gifts.

LET'S PLAN IT!

---

2 Strategies for Planning With Youth

STRATEGY 1:
Biannual Planning Retreat

Invite leaders, both youth and adults, with a ratio of about 2 youth to 1 adult. This arrangement models a partnership of youth and adults and shows that you want youth to lead from the start.

Pick a date at least 6–8 weeks ahead of time, keeping in mind school and work schedules. Try to get away to a retreat center or another church for at least one night to enhance bonding of your leadership team. Give yourself at least 5 or 6 hours of working time.

Before you leave have your youth make a master calendar to work with on your retreat. To do this use one large sheet of paper for each month you are going to plan, so you can put them all on one wall and see what your next 6 months look like.

Remind everyone to bring their personal or family calendars. Have some extras on hand to give to youth who do not have one. For some, this may be their first calendar!

Once at the retreat site do some community building. Here is an activity that is especially good for helping groups begin thinking about leadership and working together as a team—

THE NUMBERS GAME

Stand on a chair and instruct your leaders that you want them to use their bodies to form numbers 1 through 10, like a marching band. You will shout "1" and they are to form a 1 that you must be able to read. When they have made a readable 1, you will shout "2," and so on.

Before you begin, have the group come to a consensus as to how long (minutes and seconds) it will take them to do this successfully. Time them as they do the activity.

When they've finished, ask:

- How did it feel to do this activity?

- Who were the primary leaders?

- Did it take more or less time than you thought?

Then have them repeat the activity, but this time no one is allowed to talk! Once again, agree on the length of time they think it will take, then do the activity. When you are done again ask the same questions given on page 28.

Also ask:

- What was it like not to be able to talk?
- Why did it take longer (or less time) than when you could talk?
- What did you learn about leadership from this activity?

Read 1 Corinthians 12:4–11.

Ask:

- What did you learn about being the body of Christ in this activity?

Brainstorm Ideas

Service and Outreach Fundraisers

Food scavenger hunt
in neighborhood

Sell calendars

Work in soup kitchen

Rake leaves for elderly

Caroling to shut-ins

Mission trip

Christmas bake sale

Car wash

Sell pumpkins

Silent auction

Serious Topics

Undercover detective
guest speaker

Dreams

Life after death

Visit Jewish temple

Dealing with conflict

Fun Stuff

Mall tag

Parent's night skits

Secret pals

Mini golf

Bowling night

Look Ahead

Put programs on your calendar, keeping a balance of the different types of events. If you have goals for the year, work toward them as you plan.

For example: If you have a summer mission trip planned, be sure to put in enough fundraisers to raise the money you need. Also, plan some mini-mission projects so youth can get an idea of what it means to serve.

Doing long-range planning in this manner, you can keep your eye on the future. You'll have a picture of the whole year, not just one week or one month.

Assign three persons, at least one youth and one adult, to each program.

LIST THE ADULTS' NAMES IN ALL CAPITAL LETTERS ON YOUR YOUTH GROUP CALENDARS.

Look to any major events you want to plan for the next full year, such as retreats, trips, or conference events that need long-range reservations. Assign one youth and one adult to each event, along with deadlines for each event.

Practice Planning!

Do a roleplay of how two youth and an adult would meet to plan a specific event.

Have two youth and one adult sit in the middle of the group and give them an event from the calendar you just made. Have them start from the beginning, talking about what they will need to do to make this event happen. If you have a Program Preparation Form (see page 45), give them one to use. If they get stuck have them make a note but do not help them at this point!

When they are done, have the rest of the group affirm what they did well and work together to find creative solutions for where the planning group got stuck. NO NEGATIVE BASHING! Remember this is practice.

Close in Worship

Also remind everyone to be in prayer for whomever is leading a program the week before it happens. Worship should be very simple, such as—

- Opening Song—"Sanctuary" (<u>Youth! Praise 2</u>)
- Scripture—1 Samuel 3:1–10
- Prayer—Ask a youth ahead of time to write this or lead the litany given on page 22. The prayer should celebrate the time you've spent together and the team's commitment and dedication.
- Closing Song—"Hey Now" (<u>Songs From the Loft</u>, by Amy Grant and friends)

Follow Up!

Put all planning on a master calendar and mail it to everyone involved. It's also a good idea to give copies to the church secretary, parents, and your pastor!

STRATEGY 2:
The 6-Week Planning Cycle

Set a date for your first meeting and decide where and what time to have it. Scheduling the meeting during a regular youth-group time may allow maximum attendance. Holding it in someone's home may make everyone more comfortable.

Have everyone bring calendars. Bring a church calendar of all church events that the youth want to be a part of.

Brainstorm ideas (see page 30). If necessary to get things started, be ready with some of your own.

As you put events on the calendar, be sure to balance the types of things you want to do—fundraisers, serious topics, fun stuff, and service ideas.

Assign a leadership team of two to three persons to be in charge of each event. List their names on the calendar.

Set your next date and look at any dates down the road.

Do a leadership training exercise (see page 27) or learn a skill (see page 33) as part of your meeting.

Close with worship (see page 34).

Assign someone to put the youth events on the church calendar and to give that information to everyone involved.

FINGER TOUCH CIRCLE

Stand in a circle touching fingertips with those of the people on your right and left. While staying connected and using only your fingertips, try to exercise power and feel the power of the others by gently pressing and releasing your fingertips. After a minute or so, stop. Ask: "What was that like?" "Were you able to exert power over those next to you?" "What does this activity say to us as leaders?"

BEAN EXCHANGE

Give each person in your group 10 beans. Say: "For the next 3 minutes go around and GIVE as many beans away as you can." After they have done this, say: "Now, try (nonviolently!) to GET as many beans as you can." After a few minutes, stop.

Ask: "What was it like to give away your beans?" "What was it like to try to take beans from others?" "Which one were you most successful at?" "What does this activity say to us as leaders?" "How will our actions influence others?"

LET'S LEAD IT!

7 Important Traits of Leadership

Leadership is nurtured and grown with ongoing training and recruitment of youth and adults who have the following characteristics of potential leaders.

1 Forward Looking

Youth and adults who can see farther than the end of their noses are potential leaders.

Signs of a forward-looking person:

- Thinking about colleges or possible careers after high school.

- Dreaming about what youth group could look like.

In other words, **No "But we've always done it that way before!"**

2 Hopeful and Positive

The last thing you need is someone on your leadership team who drags your youth ministry down by constantly complaining.

Signs of a hopeful and positive person:

- Talking about their own future with excitement.
- Looking for creative solutions, rather than bemoaning the problem.

In other words, **No Whiners!**

3 High Commitment

When other youth see that their peers are excited and will work hard as leaders, it inspires everyone in your youth ministry.

Signs of high commitment:

- Getting homework or chores done without being told
- Having a calendar
- Being active in extracurricular activities at school

In other words, **No Slackers!**

4 Eager to Learn & Improve

All leaders make mistakes. The good ones admit their slip-ups and learn from them.

Signs of being eager to learn and improve:

- Openly admitting mistakes, without putting themselves or others down.
- Desiring to go to training events.
- Willingly doing a new activity.
- Reading the newspaper or watching the news regularly.

In other words, **No Excuses.**

5 Humble Yet Confident

Leadership is a gift from God. You can either be thankful for it and use it to help bring about the Kingdom of God or abuse it to manipulate others.

Signs of being humble yet confident:

- Not having to take personal credit all the time.
- Willingly teaching others how to lead, without putting anyone down.
- Taking on new projects.

In other words, **No Fear.**

6 Ability to Build Relationships

You can tell much about leaders by their followers.

(Adapted from an old Native American saying.)

Leaders who do not know their people are of little use.

Signs of ability to build relationships:

- Greeting new persons in the group.
- Being concerned about others in the group.
- Sitting in the middle of worship, not on the edges.

In other words, **No Loners.**

7 SPIRITUAL OPENNESS AND DEPTH

Bill Easum, a resource leader on church growth, says that our goal in the church should be to build spiritual redwoods!

Signs of spiritual openness and depth are:

- Reading the Bible regularly.
- Regularly attending Sunday school.
- Not judging others' faith as immature.
- Talking with others about faith and why it's important.

In other words, **No Spiritual Lilliputians!**

12 Hints to Keep Your Ministry Youth-Led and Youth-Planned

1 Build Relationships Between Youth and Adults by . . .

- Taking them out to lunch in groups of two or three.
- Going on a retreat with only your adults for bonding time.
- Developing a prayer phone chain for when a youth or adult is in need.
- Doing community-building games before your meetings that help youth and adults get to know each other better.
- Visiting homes of youth and adult leaders when possible.
- Building in quality one-on-one time with your leaders.

2 Develop a Plan for Training

For example, meet once every other month over dinner.

3 Evaluate

Use a standard form and keep the evaluations on file so leaders can refer to them for future planning.

SAMPLE
Youth Program Evaluation Form

Program Title:_____

Circle one: Junior High   Senior High   Both

Date of Program:_____

Today's Date:_____

Your Name (optional):_____

What was the most effective part of the program and why?

What was the least effective part of the program and why?

How can we make it better next time?

If you were the leader of this program,
    What would you do differently next time?
    What did you learn?

4 Get Parents Involved

Parents can help with details, such as fundraisers, driving, and food. That way your leaders will have less to worry about.

5 Use a Program Preparation Reminder

Several weeks before an event, send the leaders a checklist of what needs to be done in order to plan and carry out that program.

SAMPLE

Youth Program Preparation List

Circle one: Junior High   Senior High   Both

Event or Title of Program:

Date of Program: Time of Program:

Youth Leader(s):

Adult Leader(s):

Approximate number of youth who will attend:

Do you need a sign-up? If so, by when?

Do you need a speaker?

If so, how far ahead will you need to call to line up the speaker(s)?

What resources will you need for the event?

Check with _____ or look in the youth program shelves in the youth room for ideas.

Will you need any special items or materials?

Check the supply cupboard. Call _____ to approve any purchases beforehand.

Do you need to reserve a room or equipment?

Will any youth group money be needed, or will youth need to bring money? If so, how much?

Contact _____ if you need any help or assistance with your program. Remember you are in charge; don't be afraid to delegate tasks to other youth and get them involved!

Put any other notes or comments about the program on the reverse side of this form and turn it in to _____. This will be used in the future for planning, so it's important you keep good notes.

THANKS FOR YOUR HARD WORK!

6 Use a Clipboard

Keep all the notes together. Then give the clipboard to a youth volunteer to

- Make announcements for upcoming events and who's in charge;
- Ask for joys and concerns for prayer;
- Take attendance or record any other important information.

SAMPLE
From the Clipboard

YOUTH HAPPENINGS TODAY
2:30–5:30 PM—Jr. High at the Soup Kitchen
6:00–8:00 PM—Sr. High program on "Holiday Depression"

NEXT SUNDAY
1:00 PM—Youth MALT
6:00–8:00 PM—Sr. High CLIFF groups
6:00–8:00 PM—Jr. High Bible Trivia. Braden and Sam in charge.

SATURDAY & SUNDAY, FEBRUARY 1 & 2 - Snow Weekend!
Join us for a great weekend of skiing and playing ...You don't have to be a skier to go! Registrations are due December 15 with a $25 deposit. Don't miss out! Get your registration form now!

List—

JOYOUS THANGZ   SAD THANGZ

7 Have All Ages on Your Youth Leadership Team

This way you nurture leadership in younger youth and avoid losing all your leaders in one year!

8 Help Youth Succeed

Help youth think things through ahead of time. Practice with them if need be. Be a coach! However, if something fails use the experience as a learning opportunity. Help the planners or leaders think through what they might have done differently.

9 Use These Leading Steps:

- I lead it. You watch me and ask questions after.
- We lead it together. Then we talk about how it went.
- You lead it; I watch. Then we talk about how it went.
- You lead it. You look for other potential leaders; I go help someone else!

10 Remember the 80% Rule

If someone can do it 80% as well as you can, train them to do it and you go do something else. Don't wait for 100%, because no one can ever do it as well ("the same way") as you can!

11 Never Stop Encouraging Your Youth!

Always pump them up and remind them they are doing a good job! They need your love and support at all times, especially when they fail.

12 Pray Regularly for Your Youth and Adult Leaders

—and let them know you are doing it! Never forget that we are about ministry—doing God's work in the world—not simply about developing leaders.

A goal for any youth ministry is

to help young people understand

they are **children of God,**

and as such they are loved by God

and called to offer

the good news of Christ

to the world!

TROUBLESHOOTING

11 Common Problems and Prescriptions to Cure Them!

1 Need More Congregational Support

Get youth up front more in worship. Try to avoid being limited to one youth Sunday a year. Get youth involved on a regular basis as ushers and greeters, or in doing silly announcements about upcoming youth programs, or acting out parables.

2 Need More Parental Support

Do a parents night in the program where parents come and participate in the youth group. Also plan programs to support parents and encourage dialogue between parents and youth. Involve parents in planning when possible. Consider a Parent Council to provide these services:

- Host regular meetings to discuss any major upcoming youth programs, to coordinate driving for youth events, and to set long-term dates. All parents are invited.

- Set up one major parents meeting at the beginning of each school year to welcome and orient new parents.

- Advocate for parents of youth. Their needs may include events specifically for parents or for parents and youth together.

- Approve permission slips, medical release forms, a driving policy, and any other forms that need parental signatures.

3 Need More Support From Your Pastor

Invite your pastor to come and be "interviewed" by the youth group or to lead a youth group meeting or class in an area where he or she has some expertise. Keep the pastor informed about what the youth are doing and thinking. Include him or her in planning meetings. Talk over any concerns. Help your pastor get to know youth, both as the group and as individuals.

4 Trapped in Thinking Youth Leadership Must Look a Certain Way

Affirm what is unique about your church and your youth ministry. Remember that all churches have different gifts, which come from the same Source. Also know that there is no magic formula for youth ministry, and while a small church's youth ministry may look different from a large church's, it's still about doing the work of God!

5 Don't Know Where to Find Youth Ministry Resources

 There are many places to find helpful tools for youth ministry. Here are just a few:

Cokesbury 800-672-1789; Curric-U-Phone 800-251-8591
Group Publishing—also offers regional training events
Youth Specialties—also offers regional training events
Bi-Annual Youth Worker's FORUM
Perkins School of Youth Ministry, Dallas, Texas

6 Apathy in Your Youth

Start with where they are and work things in gradually. If the older youth just won't take leadership roles, then slowly work on younger youth. Also, consider how you might do things differently, so you're really touching their hearts and not just doing programs.

7 But Our Youth Are Already Too Busy!

Some are, but many are not. It's often the unpopular or unbusy youth who need the church, because it may be the only place they have to develop their leadership skills. And don't forget that even busy people need spiritual food!

8 Help, I'm About to Burn Out and Fade Away

Devotional prayer time and finding support from other youth workers are important. Develop a relationship with your staff parish or personnel committee that can support you and seek out a few people in your church who are encouraging. Visit them frequently! Don't spend your energy on those who nag at you. Finally, have other things in your life besides working with youth to keep things in perspective. That is to say, GET A LIFE!

9 This is More Work Than Doing It All Myself!

It can be in the short term. But in the long run it's less work, because you are training and enabling others to do work that you are now doing. Look at it as a long-term investment. It takes 6 months to a year to see the fruits of your labor, so find mini-successes and celebrate them whenever you can.

10 Adult Leaders Don't Know Their Youth

Be sure you get adult volunteers who will spend time with youth. Encourage your adults to go to lunch at your youth's schools or to their athletic events or choir concerts. Once adults have made it known to youth that they are interested, they will get lots of invitations.

Mission trips and other overnight events are also when great connections happen between youth and adults. There is nothing like spending a week together in serving others to grow relationships.

It also can be helpful to do a "Favorite Night," where youth and adults share their favorite music, movies, vacations, and so on, and tell why.

11 Our Youth Minister Is Always Changing

Take care of your youth minister for it can often be a thankless job! Help build support for him or her by encouraging them to take time off, go to youth training events, and lobby for an appropriate salary and bonuses (if they are paid.) Finally, developing a team of people to lead your youth ministry is your best insurance for stability and continuity.

P.S.—It's not the paid staff person's job to do all the ministry; rather, his or her job is to train and encourage others—youth and adults—to be in ministry.

Mini - Workshop

FOR LEADERS

Leadership Training for Youth and Adults

Work with several youth and adults to help you lead this workshop. **You will be modeling what you are teaching.**

Leadership as the Body

minutes

- OPENING DEVOTION 5–8
  Song (perhaps "We Believe in God," by Amy Grant)
  Scripture reading (1 Corinthians 12:14–26)
  Prayer (Ask a youth ahead of time.)

- WHO ARE WE, ANYWAY? 10–15
  Four Corner Nametags (page 60)

- WE ARE THE BODY! 25–35
  Play the game (page 61)

- WE ARE MANY GIFTS! 10–15
  Take the test (page 63)

- WHAT GIFTS ARE WE? 10–15
  Talk about your discoveries (page 68)

- CAN PEOPLE WITH DIFFERENT GIFTS
  WORK TOGETHER? 20–30
  Roleplay and discuss (page 69)

- YES! WE CAN—AS THE BODY OF CHRIST! 15–25
  Thank You, God (page 70)
  Holy Communion and hymn

Who Are We, Anyway?

Four Corner Nametags

Give everyone a large index card and have them write his or her name in the middle. Then in each of the four corners, have them write:

- A word or two that describes youth for them.

- The name of an adult who was/is important to them as a youth.

- An event from their youth that is significant.

- The name of a youth who is important to them.

Have the group split into pairs and talk about their nametags. Then have partners introduce each other to the group.

We Are the Body!

Create a Body with individuals as its parts: Eyes, Mouth (one person each); Ears, Hands, Feet (two persons each). (If the group is small, one player can be two body parts.) The Eyes can only see, Ears can only hear, and so on; so everyone is blindfolded except the Eyes.

The object is for Body's parts to work together and perform certain tasks before Life dies, signified by a timer set for 30 minutes. The Body can save Life if it completes the tasks before the timer rings.

Have youth put the blindfolds on. Set the timer and give the Body its first task (written on a slip of paper). Give it to the Eyes, who whisper it to the Ears, who whisper it to the Mouth, who speaks it out loud to the rest of the Body.

When the Body must go somewhere, the Feet must carry the Eyes (who can see), and the remaining parts of the Body must follow in a single-file line, holding onto each others' waists. In this case the Eyes may speak in order to give directions to the rest of the Body.

**Here are some examples of tasks for the body.
Feel free to make up your own!**

● The Hands, guided by the Eyes, must feed crackers and juice to the Mouth. The Feet then carry the Eyes to a designated place, followed by the rest of the Body in single-file.

● The Hands must splint and bandage one arm and one leg on both of the Feet, guided by the Eyes, Ears, and Mouth.

● The Body must find an envelope containing a key. Then it must use the key to open a box or door, guided by the Eyes, Ears, and Mouth and carried there by the Feet.

Afterward ask questions about the game:
  • How did each part of the body function?
  • How did everyone do his or her part?
  • Why did some people not get involved?

Relate this experience to Paul's analogy of the body (1 Corinthians 12:14–26).

We Are Many Gifts!

Discover Your Spiritual Gifts Test
Next to each statement, write the number that most applies to you—

3 = That's ME!
2 = This is PROBABLY me.
1 = This is PROBABLY NOT me.
0 = DEFINITELY NOT me!

_____ 1. I try to worry more about the needs of others than my own.

_____ 2. People come to me when they need to talk out a problem.

_____ 3. I would like to give money to those in need.

_____ 4. I enjoy explaining the Bible to others.

_____ 5. I like to try to help others know God better.

_____ 6. I don't mind being seen with people who aren't that popular.

_____ 7. When I see needy people on cold nights, I really feel like inviting them to my home.

_____ 8. On Friday nights I am usually the one who decides where we go and what we do.

_____ 9. I like to tell others about my relationship with God.

_____ 10. I have confidence that God will get me through both good and bad times.

_____ 11. I like doing jobs that most people don't want to do.

_____ 12. I am known for my positive attitude.

_____ 13. I get a real kick out of giving stuff away.

_____ 14. I like studying the Bible so I can explain it to others.

___ 15. I like to pray for and with others.

___ 16. I would like to work with disabled people.

___ 17. I like having friends stay overnight at my house.

___ 18. I like to organize and motivate groups of people.

___ 19. I can sometimes make discussions relate to God.

___ 20. I believe that God can do things that seem impossible.

___ 21. I have helped other people so their work was easier.

___ 22. I like to help sad people feel better.

___ 23. I try to be smart with my money so that I can give extra money to people who need it.

___ 24. I like learning and studying the Bible.

___ 25. I would love to lead a Bible study at school.

___ 26. I feel very sympathetic toward the needy.

___ 27. I don't feel disrupted when there are guests at my home.

___ 28. I have encouraged others to finish a job.

___ 29. I would like to help someone else become a Christian.

___ 30. I have confidence that God will keep God's promises even when things are bad.

___ 31. I don't mind doing little jobs that other people don't consider important.

___ 32. I can encourage others through what I say.

___ 33. I know that God will meet my needs.

___ 34. I could show others what different ideas in the Bible mean.

___ 35. I like to serve people to show that God cares for them.

___ 36. If a friend is sick, I call to see how he/she is doing.

___ 37. I like having company come to my house.

___ 38. I would like to lead, inspire, and motivate people to do God's work.

___ 39. I would like to tell others that Jesus is the Savior and help them see the positive results.

___ 40. I trust that I can call on God and know that God will be there when "impossible" situations happen.

___ 41. Sometimes when I do jobs, nobody notices, but I don't mind.

___ 42. I like it when people are happier after I have talked to them.

___ 43. I have given away my money or belongings to those in need.

___ 44. I think that I could show others how to find answers on their own.

___ 45. I would like to help bring people back to Christ who have wandered away from him.

___ 46. When I see a homeless person, I really want to help.

___ 47. My friends come over to my house because they feel comfortable there.

___ 48. When I'm in a group, sometimes people look to me to take charge.

___ 49. I take any opportunity I can to tell people about Christ.

___ 50. When everything looks bad, I can still trust God.

Test Tabulation Instructions

● Put your response (0–3) to each statement in the blank
  next to the appropriate numbers on the chart below.

● Add up the numbers going across the blanks and
  record them in the box under "Total."

					Total	Gift
1___	11 ___	21___	31___	41___	___	A
2___	12 ___	22___	32___	42___	___	B
3___	13 ___	23___	33___	43___	___	C
4___	14 ___	24___	34___	44___	___	D
5___	15 ___	25___	35___	45___	___	E
6___	16 ___	26___	36___	46___	___	F
7___	17 ___	27___	37___	47___	___	G
8___	18 ___	28___	38___	48___	___	H
9___	19 ___	29___	39___	49___	___	I
10___	20___	30___	40___	50___	___	J

Explanation of Gift Letters

A **Helping** The ability to assist and serve other people.

B **Encouraging** The ability to support people and help them to regain hope.

C **Giving** The ability to give your time and money so that it can be used for God's work.

D **Teaching** The ability to teach the Bible in such a way that people can learn and grow.

E **Pastoring** The ability to effectively guide and care for people in their walk with God.

F **Mercy** The ability to act out of compassion toward those who are suffering.

G **Hospitality** The gift of being friendly and generous to guests.

H **Leading** The ability to motivate others to use their spiritual gifts and to do their best for the work of the Lord.

I **Evangelism** The ability to help others to come to know Jesus personally.

J **Faith** The ability to have the confident belief that God will always do what is the very best.

Assessment

Determine your demonstrated probable spiritual gift(s) as follows: If the score in the "Total" column is

12–15: There is great evidence that God has blessed you with this spiritual gift.

8–11: There is a strong possibility that God has blessed you with this spiritual gift.

4–7: There is a good possibility that God could be developing this gift in you.

0–4: You are spiritually gifted, probably in an area other than this one.

Taken from <u>Developing Student Leaders</u>, by Ray Johnston. Copyright © 1991 by Youth Specialties, Inc. Used by permission of Zondervan Publishing House.

WHAT GIFTS ARE WE?

Discuss the following questions.

● What gifts do you bring to your church?

● How do you use your gifts?

● What is your current role at your church?

● What would you like your role to be?

Can People With Different Gifts Work Together?

Roleplay

Photocopy the roles given below and cut them apart. Give each individual his or her role direction privately. The scene is a group of youth and adults who are planning for a new youth group. At the end of the roleplay, talk about how leadership teams can work together more effectively.

Leader: You want to organize the members into a productive group. You express yourself but do not monopolize. You work hard to get everyone excited and cooperating with one another. You keep people on track.

Supporter: You endorse constructive action and are a big help to others. You are enthusiastic about getting this new group off the ground.

Skeptic: You doubt the merits of starting this group. It's hard for you to imagine the youth coming together. You bring problems to the attention of the others.

Passive Person: You find it hard to get excited about much of anything—pro or con. You are extremely bored and speak a little contemptuously.

Joker: You make light of everything. You kid around and have fun without causing too much disturbance.

Peacemaker: You like to try to change situations for the benefit of everyone. If people are acting too negative or goofing around, you confront them; if they are bored, you attempt to get them involved.

Yes, We Can—as the Body of Christ!

Closing Devotion

Have each person complete the following statement:

"Thank you God, for the gift of _____, which you have given to me."

If possible, share in Communion together and talk about the symbolism of the Body of Christ being nourished by the common bread and the cup. Together sing "One Bread, One Body" (The United Methodist Hymnal, 620).

THE BIG PICTURE

Working with youth is a little like putting together a jigsaw puzzle: It helps to have a picture of what it's supposed to look like!

In effective youth ministry **vision** is central.

Seven major elements contribute to realizing that vision. The more of them developed and in place, the better.

Youth ministry planners in individual churches can develop each of those areas **their own way**, according to their congregation's particular resources, gifts, and priorities and the needs of their youth.

How does this SkillAbility fit in this big picture?
Here are just a few of the ways. By focusing on leadership training for both youth and adults, you

● make youth ministry a priority in your **CONGREGATION** and communicate to young people they are valued;

● create **STRUCTURES** that give youth a special way to be connected;

● work from the **PERSPECTIVE** that teenagers have gifts to be identified, encouraged, and put into ministry. You see them as partners and as leaders.

● hone their skills for going out into the **COMMUNITY** in service and as witnesses, giving others a glimpse of the Kingdom.

YOUTH MINISTRY: A COMPREHENSIVE APPROACH

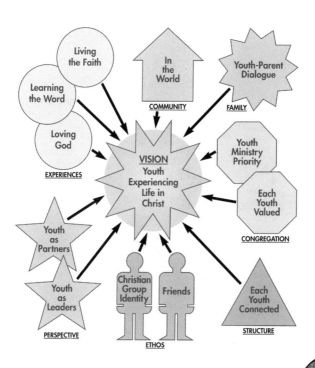

FAMILY

Research is clear that **parent-youth dialogue** about matters of faith are crucial for youth to develop mature faith. Youth themselves express desire to be listened to, to have boundaries, and to have parental involvement in their lives. Parents need skills for relating to their changing teens as well as assurance that their values and voice do matter to their youth. How do we in the church facilitate parent-youth dialogue?

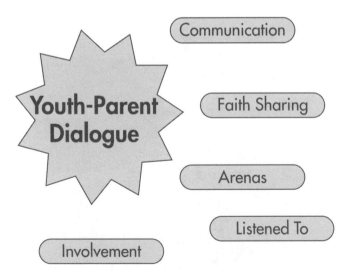

Youth-Parent Dialogue

Communication

Faith Sharing

Arenas

Listened To

Involvement

CONGREGATION

Youth ministry is the ministry of the whole congregation, beginning with making **youth ministry a priority**: prayer for the ministry, people (not just one person!), time, effort, training, resources, and funding. The goal for the congregation is **each youth valued**. Interaction with adults, including mentors, positive language about youth, prayer partners for each one, simply being paid attention to—these are active roles for the congregation.

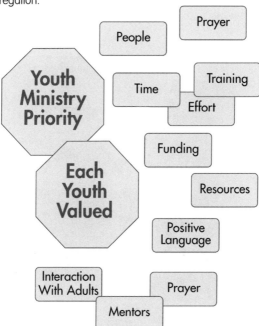

Prayer

People

Youth Ministry Priority

Time

Training

Effort

Each Youth Valued

Funding

Resources

Positive Language

Interaction With Adults

Prayer

Mentors

STRUCTURE

Whatever shape the ministry takes, the goal is to have **each youth connected.** Sunday school and youth group are only a beginning. What are the needs of the youth? What groups (even of 2 or 3), what times would help connect young people to the faith community? How easy is it for new youth to enter? How well do we stay in touch with the changing needs of our youth? Do we have structures in place that facilitate communication? outreach? "How" can vary; it's the "why" that's crucial.

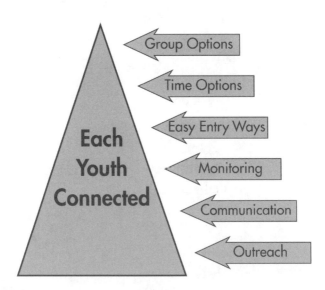

Each Youth Connected

- Group Options
- Time Options
- Easy Entry Ways
- Monitoring
- Communication
- Outreach

ETHOS

We are relational beings; we all need **friends**. The support, caring, and accountability friends provide help youth experience the love of God. As those friendships are nurtured within **Christian group identity**, young people claim for themselves a personal identity of being Christian. What language, rituals, traditions, and bonding experiences mark each grouping within the youth ministry as distinctively Christian?

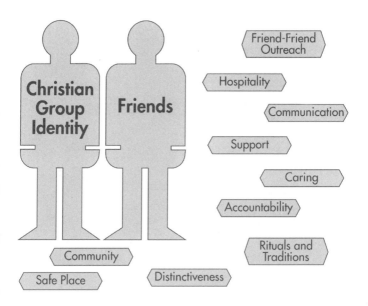

Christian Group Identity

Friends

Friend-Friend Outreach

Hospitality

Communication

Support

Caring

Accountability

Rituals and Traditions

Community

Safe Place

Distinctiveness

PERSPECTIVE

Youth are keenly aware of being considered problems, objects to be fixed, or too inexperienced to have anything to offer. What would happen if we operated from the perspective of seeing **youth as leaders, youth as partners**? We would listen to them more, be intentional about identifying their gifts, take seriously their input, encourage their decision making, and train them for leadership roles.

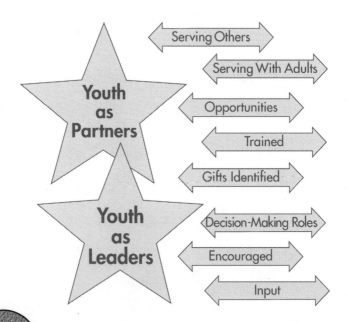

EXPERIENCES

Worship, devotions, prayer, and participation in the community of faith build for youth the experience of **loving God**. Study and reflection upon the Bible and the faith are crucial for **learning the Word**. Being among people who are Christian role models and grappling with difficult moral, ethical, justice, and stewardship issues help young people with **living the faith**. Curriculum resources specifically provide material to facilitate these three kinds of experiences.

COMMUNITY

As Christians, youth are challenged to be **in the world** as servants, as witnesses, as leaven—making a difference with their lives, giving others a glimpse of the Kingdom. What opportunities, what training, what support do we give youth to equip them for ministry beyond the walls of the church building?

In
the
World

Serving

Witnessing

Leaven/Salt/Light

Youth in Charge: How to Develop Youth Leadership